WORLD
CLIMBING
IMAGES FROM THE EDGE

SIMON CARTER

OPENING PAGES

◄ Ben Heason, *Slipstream* (E6 6a), Rainbow Slab, Llanberis, Wales, UK.

Steve Monks with Monique Forestier belaying, pitch two *Bristol Fashion* (26), Red Sail, The Grampians, Australia.

Monique Forestier, *Il N'y a D'horreur Que Dans le Nom* (7b+), Gorges du Tarn, France.

ABOVE FROM LEFT

⬆ Rachel Carr, *Travels With My Aunt* (6a), Hin Taak Wall, Phi Phi Island, Thailand.

Sean Isaac, *The Good, The Bad and The Ugly* (WI5), The Ghost, Canmore, Canada.

Fred Jabot with Nadine Rousselot belaying, *Hechizos del Viento* nine pitches (6b), on El Pisón, Riglos, Spain.

CONTENTS

FOREWORD

Rock climbing has evolved to an extraordinary degree since I took it up as a teenager in the early seventies. The once clunky and ill-fitting gear and footwear we had then has been superseded by high performance, precision tools. The climbers themselves are almost a different species: fit, flexible and athletic. Even a run-of-the-mill "good climber" today is fit enough and technically adept enough to do routes, all day long, that three decades earlier would have been twice as hard as the top route on the planet. More importantly, though, our mental outlook has taken a great leap forward, so that no one any longer declares a piece of rock to be "unclimbable," as we used to say of many stretches of cliff.

Documenting climbing's state of play, and its lifestyle into the new millennium comes Simon Carter, with his camera and his eye for the climbs and climbing feats that epitomize the way we are, as climbers, today. It seems that as long as I have known Simon — about a decade and a half — he's been freeze-framing the vital moments of a climb.

World Climbing: Images from the Edge is more than a portfolio of Simon's life work, however. It's the result of several years of globetrotting in pursuit of a visual interpretation of the elusive question "why do we climb?"

That question is the most unanswerable, and damnable thing a climber can ever be asked. Words fail whenever a climber tries to explain or justify the motivation behind this quirky, strenuous and at times risky pursuit, but Simon's photos go a long way to providing enlightenment. Looking at the images in this book, and rifling through my own vocabulary for a single word that encapsulates the mystery of why we do it, I'll venture a single word: Elation.

Greg Child
Castle Valley, Utah
September 2005

→ John Varco,
Belly Full of Bad Berries
(5.13a/b), Indian Creek,
Utah, USA.

INTRODUCTION

The World's mountains, cliffs, crags and boulders provide us with some of the most spectacular and beautiful places on earth. These inspirational settings are the scene for real adventures and extraordinarily demanding challenges, or simply for play.

Climbing provides an avenue that allows us to experience these places in a unique way. It gives us a new perspective on our lives and our world. It gives us a chance to escape the data-smog of our information-overloaded society and to reconnect with the natural world. Climbing gives us amazing opportunities.

In the early 20th century rock-climbing was seen by many climbers as little more than practice for mountaineering, but since then it has been increasingly performed as a worthwhile activity in its own right. Modern equipment, training and techniques have helped climbing to continue to evolve and diversify. Now we have many highly specialised sub-sports and different styles of climbing, all of which can be intrinsically fascinating and absorbing activities.

The skill, strength and commitment of top climbers are of such high standards that their achievements often astound us. Yet, as many of them have said, it's not simply about 'hard'. I'd say it's more about getting out there and giving it a go. Given the sheer number and range of climbing problems that exist — from the easiest rambles to the most extreme undertakings — there is a challenge for everyone. It is important though, that the challenges we set ourselves are personal ones, that we make our own decisions, and accept the risks. Anyone using this book should read and ensure they understand the warning on page 192.

In 2000, after photographing climbing for several years in Australia, I started a new personal challenge: to travel to some of the world's great climbing areas and to capture both the places and action on film. It turned into an on-going odyssey, sometimes planned, sometimes spontaneous. A chance meeting here, an invitation there, has guided my travels in the most rewarding ways. As when Will Gadd said "If you'd like to come to Canada and shoot some ice..."

Meeting and photographing many different climbers has been one of the most enjoyable aspects of my journey. The enthusiasm shown by so many has been instrumental in keeping my own energy going at times. It has also been heartening to see the climbing spirit alive and well in so many different parts of the world.

It is evident to me that climbers the world over have much in common. Though some prefer one style of climbing over another, they all revel in the fact that climbing in nature's playground is a world apart from more conventional recreation. This is not simply a sport — it's a way of life.

In some respects this book is a photographic journal of my travels through our climbing world these last few years, but it is much more than that. It has been an extraordinary journey which has left me in no doubt that climbing is a superb way to experience some of the best things in our amazing world. Above all, it is the places and the people and their passion that I celebrate.

Simon Carter

Dave Pickford soloing
Free Born Man (E4 6a),
Conner Cove, Dorset, UK.

AUSTRALIA
BLUE MOUNTAINS

Australia may not have high mountains by world standards but you'd never know this in the undeniable ruggedness of the Blue Mountains. They are not a range of jagged peaks but an elevated plateau cut by deep valleys, canyons and gullies ringed by sandstone escarpments. They begin barely eighty kilometres from Sydney where Australia was first settled by Europeans in 1788, yet it took many serious attempts spanning decades before the first white explorers could find a way through to the country out west.

Climbers are lucky. Today a highway and railway cross the mountains making them an easy two hours from the city. For many there's no need to commute as they live here instead. The tourist towns provide climbers' essentials — such as bakeries, cafes, and good restaurants. The latter are handy for celebrating the achievement of big goals — or just another great day at the crag.

The Blueys are immense. You can climb virtually in suburban backyards — or begin a day of serious adventure in World Heritage wilderness just minutes after downing the morning's latte. Some of the two thousand plus routes are over three hundred metres but most are single-pitch (up to one rope-length). There are those protected with traditional (removable) protection, but where blank walls are tackled they're usually protected with bolts. There are plentiful prime sport climbing crags, some among the best in the land. Small, sharp gritty edges give bouldery cruxes — and some of the country's hardest routes. History is still being written here, by climbers, on wildly over-hanging walls.

➜ Nigel Campbell, *Debris* (23), Pierce's Pass.

↑ Mike Law, pitch four *Red Edge* (23, 24, 22, 26, 24), Perry's Lookdown.
→ Garth Miller, *Grey Area* (33), Diamond Falls.

Steve McClure,
Super Duper Goo (29),
Diamond Falls.

Stefan Glowacz,
Soul Catcher (25),
Porter's Pass.

AUSTRALIA
GRAMPIANS

The glorious jagged ranges of the Grampians National Park extend one hundred kilometres tip to toe. The area is a three hour drive northwest from Melbourne. It is rough, rocky country crossed by few roads. The bush teems with iconic Aussie wildlife: koalas, emus, and kangaroos. Seemingly endless opportunities for great cragging are found here: there are thousands of routes and perhaps hundreds of crags — though they're rarely set up for convenience.

The Grampians' jewel is for sure Taipan Wall on Mount Stapylton at the northern end of the range. Taipan's seventy metre-high sweep of hard, almost marbled, overhanging sandstone is a most exquisite deep orange — treasured like gold by some climbers. It might seem unfair but nothing is easy on the main wall. Smooth, sloping holds combined with very spaced bolting regularly dish out big-air. However, the Stapylton area has many excellent crags encompassing an extraordinarily diverse range of climbing. There is easy and cutting-edge climbing and bouldering scattered widely around.

Heading south down the range the diversity just keeps increasing. Mount Difficult and Mount Rosea are just some of the cliffs with superb trad multi-pitching. Bundaleer near the height of the range gives shade from summer sun ensuring climbing year round. Down south in the Victoria Range it's well worth the long hike into numerous isolated crags (such as Eureka Wall, Muline, Gallery and The Fortress) for although they have only a few routes each, some are simply Australia's finest.

Lynn Hill, *Archimedes Principle* (25), Eureka Wall.

◄ David Jones,
Feather Boa (28),
Taipan Wall.

➔ Monique Forestier,
pitch two *Serpentine* (29),
Taipan Wall.

FROM TOP

↑ Chris Jones, project (30+).
David Jones, *Somoza* (32).
Nathan Hoette, *Spartacus* (33).
All on Sandinista Cliff,
Mount Stapylton.

← Malcolm Matheson,
Redline (28), The Lost World.

→ Steve Monks with Monique
Forestier belaying, pitch two
Bristol Fashion (26), Red Sail.

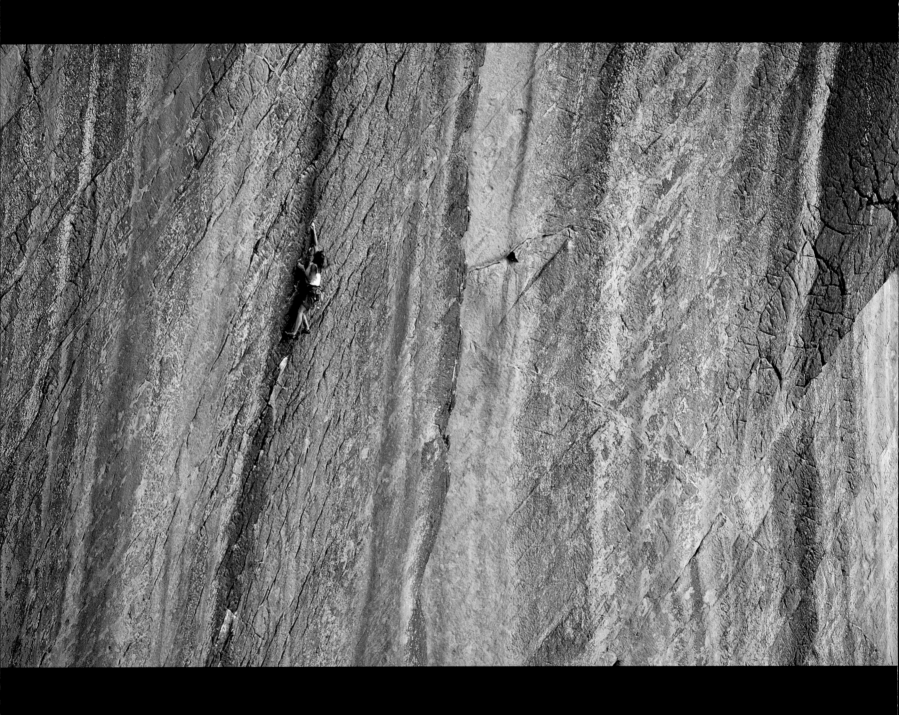

AUSTRALIA
MOUNT ARAPILES

Heading west from the Grampians the countryside flattens out into wide open expanses of wheat and sheep farms. After nearly an hour's drive an outcrop appears which at first sight resembles Uluru (Ayres Rock). It is the one last blip before Australia's Great Dividing Range peters out. Closer inspection reveals this kilometre-long outcrop to be a complex network of cliffs, crags, buttresses and gullies, packing in far more climbing than might be imagined. It is called Mount Arapiles and has over two thousand routes.

The ultra-hard rock is a joy to behold — and fondle and crimp. Pressure and heat has produced quartzose sandstone with smooth bulges dubbed 'bum rock'. There is sport climbing at higher grades but trad is the trump card. The easy routes are truly world-class and perhaps unrivalled for refining the art; they feature fissures for bomber placements, chicken-heads and jugs galore.

Onsighting harder routes is unexpectedly tricky not only because hanging around placing gear is pumpy. Cruxes present technical problems of three dimensional movement and thinking: their secrets are often only revealed to climbers who've slumped onto the end of their rope.

Climbers come here for months and pick from 'The Pines' or 'The Gums' for setting up camp. It is not quite as carefree as it used to be, thanks to 'user pays', but Arapiles remains the spiritual and cultural home of Oz climbing. Many take up residence in Natimuk — a mini-metropolis nearby where their booming numbers have sent house prices soaring. It's a good place for lifers.

FROM TOP
↗ Bard Buttress and The Bluffs.
Rest day at The Pines.
Huw Widdowson, *Scourge* (20), Central Gully.

→ Tony Barron,
Agamemnon (10),
The Atridae.

◄ Lynn Hill, **Birdman of Alcatraz** (23), Death Row Pinnacle.
◤ Michael "Muki" Woods, **Cliffhanger** (25), Curtain Wall.
⬆ Julian Saunders, **India** (28), The Pharos.

Previous page: Dave Jones, **On The Prowl** (28), The Bluffs.

⬆ Monique Forestier, **Kachoong** (21), The Northern Group.

Lynn Hill, **_Debutante's and Centipedes_** (25), The Atridae.

Julian Saunders, **_Slopin' Sleazin_** (28), The Pharos.

AUSTRALIA
TOTEM POLE

Less than six metres wide at the base and over sixty metres high, this free-standing dolerite column is as improbable as it is alluring. First climbed as an aid route in 1968, the Totem Pole saw but a handful of ascents over the following decades. The two-pitch **Free Route** was established in 1995 and a variant first pitch (**Deep Play**) added a few years later. The quality of the climbing is surprisingly very good. However, an involved approach combined with frequently poor conditions and rough swells are just some of the factors that make this a more committing and serious undertaking than the grade of the climbing suggests. There is a range of interesting climbing to be found on Tasmania's Tasman Peninsular but the Tote has unique appeal.

↗ Nancy Feagin abseiling in for an attempt on the *Free Route*.

➡ Nancy Feagin preparing a 'hanging belay' just above a rough swell.

CANADA

CANADIAN ROCKIES

In summer the Canadian Rockies are home to an assortment of fine climbing locations offering a wide range of styles. But there are climbers who eagerly await the onset of winter here. When temperatures start plummeting towards minus 20 degrees Celsius they dream of extraordinary formations growing fatter — drip by drip — to create their new season's wonderland.

The range of winter climbing includes full-commitment alpine epics, single and multi-pitch routes up frozen waterfalls and ice-flows, and new-vogue mixed climbs. Mixed (rock and ice) climbing has continued to evolve and now drytooling has become an art unto itself — like a funky winter version of technical sport-climbing but with crampons and axes. The gear and techniques are barely recognisable from ten years ago. It might seem strange to climb ten or twenty metres of overhanging rock to reach a small patch of ice, but it's just another way to make the most of a magnificent winter playground.

FROM TOP

↗ Kim Csizmazia and Will Gadd approach the Stanley Headwall.

Sean Isaac climbing an ice pillar at Haffner Creek.

A view across Waterfowl Lake from the Icefields Parkway.

Eric Dumerac about to be hit by falling ice, pitch three **Louise Falls** (WI5), Lake Louise.

Kim Csizmazia soloing on **Whimper Wall** (WI4), Icefields Parkway.
Will Gadd, **Phyllis Diller** (M10), with icicles over one metre high, Stanley Headwall.

For climbers, just driving to the west coast Canadian town of Squamish has its own hazards... it is easy to be distracted by the huge granite walls of the Stawamus Chief towering above!

The Stawamus Chief really is a big wall. There are routes here of major significance in the history of North American big-wall climbing — and the area retains that importance to this day. The sweeping granite wall offers ultra-classic hard routes ten pitches long: it's primarily slab, crack and face free-climbing, though there are major aid routes here too.

Whilst The Chief is the most striking feature of the landscape, there is actually a lot more climbing to be found. Numerous smaller crags in the area have a range of both trad and sport-climbing. And there are many climbers who come here just to crank-out on the abundant boulders, often well hidden in the forest. All this adds up to a major destination with a surprising variety of climbing.

FROM LEFT

⬆ Abby Watkins, pitch four (5.9) *Grand Wall* (10 pitches, 5.11a), Stawamus Chief.
Sean Isaac, the **Split Pillar** pitch (5.10b), pitch six **Grand Wall**.

← Matt Maddaloni, pitch six
(12a) **Black Dyke** (13b),
Stawamus Chief.

→ Andrew Wexler with
Evan Stevens belaying,
pitch 11 **Freeway**
(12 pitches, 5.11d),
Stawamus Chief.

CROATIA

KORNATI
ARCHIPALEGO

As soon as climbers learn and refine a new style of climbing they start searching for new places to do it. So since Deep-Water Soloing took off it is no surprise that the Kornati Archipelago along the Croatian coast has been explored. Local climbers discovered several areas and leading practitioners of the style from other countries have made trips here — finding a DWS paradise.

With over three hundred islands in the Archipelago it can be hard to know where to start. However, excellent quality limestone cliffs have been discovered along the western edge of the Archipelago. The group pictured here climbed over fifty new up-routes and traverses in twelve days — ranging from easy to as hard as they get. Action was focused on the Islands of Mana, Panitula and Rasip, though this may be only just scratching the surface.

Cruising the Adriatic in speedboats or yachts can be an exciting adventure, but reliance on such things, and weather, can create hassles. Still, on a warm day it makes for excellent fun. Just pick a line from the boat, get dropped off, climb until you plummet, then swim...

→ Leo Houlding,
Living the Dream (7b+),
Rasip Island.

↖ Tim Emmett, *The Shrubbery* (7c+), Holy Grail Wall.

← Monique Forestier, Jess Corrie and Bean Sopwith on a sea-level traverse, Mana Island.

→ Leo Houlding, project, Panitula Island.

⬆ Steve McClure making the first ascent of *Ring of Fire* (8b+), Holy Grail Wall, Mana Island.

➡ Steve McClure attempting *Ring of Fire*.

Charlie Woodburn and Tim Emmett leap from cliffs on Mana Island.

Sunset from the village of Vruje, Kornati Island.

CZECH REPUBLIC
ADRŠPACH

Adršpach (Teplicko-Adršpašské skály), located in northeast Czech Republic, is a most notable area comprising numerous cliffs and towers, with well over two thousand routes. Climbing here has a fascinating history (it began in the 1920's) and an exceptionally pure set of climbing ethics have evolved which greatly assist preservation of the soft sandstone.

Metal protection is not allowed in cracks, hence the use of knotted ropes and slings, the making and placing of which has become a fine art. New routes are established and existing ones are all climbed 'ground up' (meaning no bolting from abseil and generally no top-roping). The special bolts are usually placed no closer than five metres apart. And chalk is not usually used. These ethics are clearly defined and most climbers abide by them. It has created a legacy of some extremely serious and challenging routes and a breed of very bold local climbers to match.

Rather than sport climbing, try the old Adršpach speciality — Support Climbing. This involves one climber standing on the shoulders of another to progress up a climb. It is known as Combined Support Climbing when three climbers work together in this way. Amazing feats of Tower Jumping are also practiced here. Originally jumping was just done on some descents (due to lack of anchors on top of some towers) but it has evolved into its own sub-sport with its own grading system (1 to 5).

◤ Adam Práza making
a grade 2 jump,
Adršpach Ostrov.

➡ Miroslav Mach,
Zasle Casy (Czech grade
VIIIa, French 6b+).

↑ Miroslav Mach, *Zasle Casy*.

↗ Miroslav Mach placing knotted-rope protection on *Kruhová Varianta* (Czech grade VIIa, French 6a).

➡ Chramove and Martinske Walls.

← Miroslav Mach, *Previsla* (Czech grade VIIIa, French 6b+).
◄ Some of the 800 or so towers in the area.
↑ A team using 'support climbing' tactics.

⬆ Miroslav Mach, *Kruhová Varianta* (Czech grade VIIa).

➡ Lubos Mazl, *Bod Zlomu* (Czech grade Xc, French 8a+), Chrámové Steny (The Church Walls).

FRANCE
CEUSE

In the mid 1980's rumours of a fantastic new alpine crag in the south of France permeated through the climbing world. Stunning new sport-routes on immaculate limestone were apparently being established by some of the country's foremost climbers, but it was their secret play thing and its location remained a mystery for some time.

Well... the cat's long out of the bag now. And the Ceuse Massif has become widely regarded as one of the finest sport-climbing crags in the world. It is home to some of the most famous, coveted and talked-about sport-routes anywhere. Yet it is an extensive crag full of surprises. Widely-spaced bolting enhances excitement, but thankfully the steep blank-looking walls often suddenly reveal deep pockets just when failing forearms need them the most. There are simply superb multi-pitch routes and some single-pitch routes extend to seventy metres.

The Massif is snow-capped in winter and commonly catches summer storms. A longish uphill grind makes for the approach. But this is a crag which speaks of quality more than convenience.

⬆ The Ceuse Massive in the Haute Alpes.
↗ Hiking up to the cliffs.
➡ François Petit, **Rosanna** (8a), La Cascade.

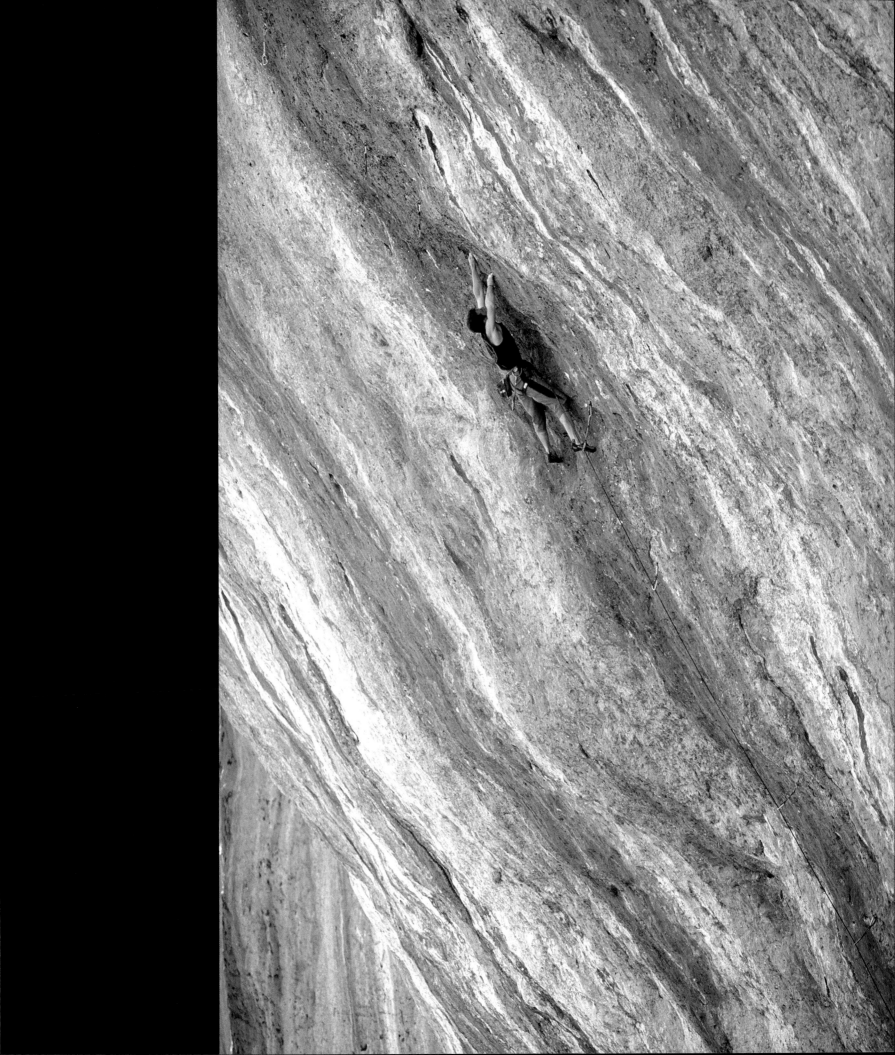

⬆ Monique Forestier with Nadine Rousselot belaying, pitch three *Inespérance* (6a+, 6b+, 6c+, 7a), Grande Face.

↗ Pitch four *Inespérance*.

➡ Chris Sharma, *No Future* (8c+), a 70 metre pitch on Biographie wall.

Previous page: François Petit,
Galoxie (7b+), Berlin wall.

◄ Nadine Rousselot, pitch three
Inespérance, Grande Face.

► Chloé Minoret, **Blanches
fesses** (7c), Sector Cascade.

FRANCE
GORGE DU TARN

Connoisseurs of premium sport-climbing will appreciate the steep sweeping pocketed limestone walls of Le Gorge du Tarn. Its many separate buttresses sprinkled throughout the gorge combine to give a choice of several hundred routes — covering a wide range of difficulties. The wise will know that not all finger pockets are created equal and will be wary for the odd finger-shredder. Experts will relish the rope-stretching pitches (up to seventy metres) and will hope they have tenacity to match. Whizzes wishing for some multi-pitching will be happy to pop around the corner to the Gorges de la Jonte. Anyone can appreciate le Tarn.

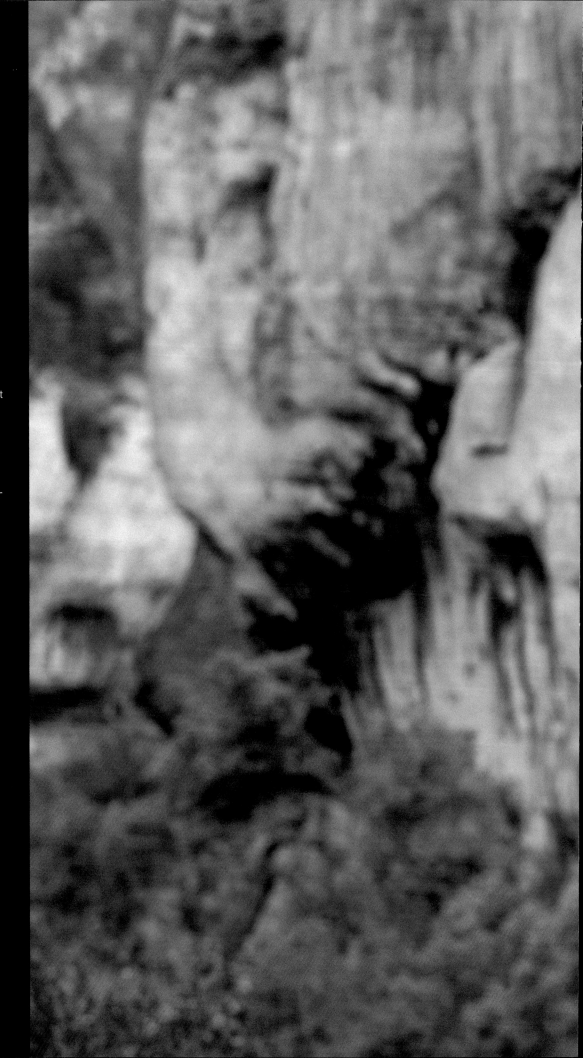

Liv Sansoz, *Bouton* (7a+),
Tennessee Wall.

Monique Forestier,
Ya Qua! (7c),
Dromadaire.

Liv Sansoz, *Octopus*
(7c+), Güllich.

FRANCE
VERDON GORGE

The immaculate three hundred metre limestone walls of Verdon Gorge are considered by many to offer multi-pitch climbing second to none. The longest routes here are approached from the bottom of the Gorge — ground up — which is a more gradual approach to savouring its exceptionally airy ambience. The entire evolution of modern free climbing has been practiced on these big cliffs at some time — leaving a legacy of long aid and trad climbs. Bolt protected routes predominate today but the bolts are widely-spaced — almost as if the exceptional exposure wasn't enough on its own.

Most of the climbing here isn't approached from the bottom of the gorge however, but from the top, by abseil. Some of the single-pitch routes at the top of the Gorge are simply superb. These are a great way to get a quick dose of the exposure and some of the finest rock. Top-down access does not necessarily mean reduced commitment however. You can abseil down to enormous ledges only part way down the cliff — and still have seven pitches of climbing to get back to the top. Stories of abseiling epics (and disasters) abound and severe summer storms don't care whether you're five pitches down, or just one.

There is some single-pitch sport-climbing around here with a walk-in approach. But it is not possible to enjoy what makes this one of the world's great classic 'crags' without sooner or later having to confront — and maybe savour — the exquisite exposure.

◪ Arnaud Petit atop the gorge.
▣ Stéphanie Bodet, pitch four
  Surveiller ét Punir (7a).

➜ Arnaud Petit,
Eve Line (7b),
Barre de l'Escales.

⬆ Arnaud Petit, *Papy on Sight* (7c+), Carelle.

➡ Stéphanie Bodet, pitch four *Surveiller ét Punir* (7a).

ITALY
ARCO

In Northern Italy the Sarca Valley extends north from Lake Garda offering dozens of different crags with over two thousand routes. The area's centre-piece is the town of Arco, home to great cafes, a vibrant local scene and more climbing shops than you can poke a stick at.

As with so many other big areas, it would be a mistake to classify the climbing here as being of only one style. This region is a single-pitch sport-climbing paradise, but there are larger cliffs further up the valley where the range of climbing opens up. There is trad and multi-pitch climbing abounds. A few routes at Placche Zebrata extend up to six hundred metres.

Some climbers come here when the weather turns bad in the nearby Dolomites or Alps and beyond. Some come to watch the annual Arco Rockmasters competition. But most just come here because the climbing is great.

Cristian Brenna, *Abissi* (7c), Massone.

➜ Cristian Brenna,
pitch three (7b) *Land
Art* (4 pitches, 7c),
Transatlantico.

Cristian Brenna, *Reini's Vibos* (8c), Massone.

Monique Forestier, *La Nonna Va* (6c+), Nago.

NEW ZEALAND
CASTLE HILL

The boulders and tors scattered around Castle Hill in central South Island have long been considered a significant climbing area. However, since the popularity of bouldering has exploded and climbers have increasingly turned their attention to the smaller stones, this area has been rediscovered — and found to be extraordinarily extensive. Some say over fourteen thousand different problems have been climbed. The high-quality limestone is riddled with pockets and slopers leading to rounded mantle finishes — making for some very intriguing problems.

FROM TOP
▸ Simon Stevens, *Opium* (V7), Spittle Hill.
Exodus of pad-people from Quantum Field.
Chris Webb, *Symptoms of Slow Twitch Motion* (V10), Quantum Field.

➜ James Kassay,
Tuppi-Master (V7),
Spittle Hill.

◄ James Kassay, **The Phoenix** (V7), Quantum Field.
◤ Dave Taylor, **Cepasa** (V4), Spittle Hill.
⬆ James Kassay, **Everything Gone Green** (V11), Quantum Field.

SPAIN

GRANADA

Climbers from the sunny Spanish town of Granada can take advantage of convenient access to many great crags in the south of the country. Some are well known — while many are not. Like climbers in other parts of this country, locals are sometimes spoilt for choice. There's really not much need for talented Granadan climbers to travel far though, when they have sport-climbing on quality limestone just minutes from home.

◪ Javier Morales, project (approx. 8c+).

→ Mariona Marti,
Titulo Ferretero (7b+).

SPAIN
RIGLOS

The massive conglomerate domes which tower above the village of Riglos in Northern Spain offer a unique climbing experience on most unusual rock. Whereas conglomerate often consists of pebbles and small stones cemented together, the rock at Riglos contains football sized stones. Where these large stones jut out from the cliff they make for great handholds, if not improbable and unnerving ones!

Some of the routes extend to over three hundred metres. The climbing is steep with long steadily overhanging sections common. Long run-outs abound — even on the bolted routes. The vultures circling above are a reminder of how committing the long multi-pitch routes can be. When the evil evening wind starts up it's best to be well on the way back to the bar.

⇥ Conglomerate domes rising behind the village of Riglos, with El Macizo del Pisón centre-left and La Visera far right.

⬆ Fred Moix, pitch four (7a) *Tucán Ausente* (seven pitches, 7a), El Macizo del Pisón.

➡ Nigel Campbell, pitch seven *La Fiesta de los Biceps* (6a+, 6b, 7a, 6c, 6c, 6c, 6c+, 6b, 3), La Visera.

➡ Monique Forestier, pitch eight *La Fiesta de los Biceps*.

Climbers on pitch
five of **Supercrak**
(8 pitches, 7a/b),
La Visera.

Simon Tappin with
Nina Leonfellner
belaying, pitch eight
Norte (8 pitches, 6b),
El Puro.

The Berne Oberland is a major area for traditional mountaineering. Climbers come to this region in the north western Swiss Alps and use the village of Grindelwald, near Interlaken, as a base for attempts on classic alpine peaks. The impressive classic trio of the Eiger, Mönch and Jungfrau is predominant. The infamous Eiger with its notorious North Face also has less serious and less difficult routes such as the classic Mittellegi Ridge. And there are numerous other grand objectives around such as Schreckhorn, Gross Fiescherhorn and Gross Grünhorn. These are serious alpine summits involving glacier travel, crossing crevasses, and climbing on snow and ice. Some of the routes have incredibly loose rock. They rise to around four thousand metres and catch the worst of the weather.

Many rock climbers also come to the area but without any interest in the higher peaks, just looking for high-quality rock. The Englehorner group is a premium choice for long multi-pitching on rock, though this usually involves a night in a hut. For those wanting to get in-and-out in a day then Hintisberg is the go, with up to five pitches of technical climbing, mostly bolted, on limestone. When finished abseil back down to the grassy meadow, lie down in comfort, soak up the sun, and enjoy the superb panorama. Try to make out the Eiger's White Spider and dream — or just be content where you are...

⬆ Cow on patrol with Hintisberg behind.
⬈ Tom Hoffman and Fred Moix scope the route.

➡ Tom Hoffman, pitch three *Spectacolo* (160 metres, 7b), with the Eiger (centre), Mönch and Jungfrau in the distance.

SWITZERLAND
RAWYL

The sunny Rhône Valley in south-west Switzerland is central to an abundance of good climbing. And when winter snow recedes from the nearby hills, options really open up. Then local climbers from the town of Sion head up to Rawyl where they'll find a pretty lake surrounded by numerous limestone walls hosting mid-grade to ultra-hard climbs, mostly protected by bolts.

Climbing began here in the early 80's and there was another wave of development in the late 90's. There are about two hundred one-pitch and fifty multi-pitch routes — some of which extend to three hundred metres. It's a significant area, just not as widely known as some.

↗ Didier Berthod, *La Nuit Grave* (8b).
→ Bottom and opposite: Didier Berthod, *Le Voile de Maya* project (approx. 8c+).

SWITZERLAND
SUSTENPASS

Less than an hour's drive east from Interlaken the road climbs to where it crosses Switzerland's Central Alps at Sustenpass. Being Switzerland, and the Alps, it's no surprise there's classic alpine climbing around here. There are also some mighty objectives for those with a penchant for technical rock climbing.

To the north of the pass, Titlis rises to an altitude of over three thousand metres. When conditions are good the huge walls of this mountain peak have long multi-pitching, the difficulty of which is as hard as anyone would want. Take, for example, the five hundred metre **Last Exit Titlis** which is one of the hardest modern long routes in Europe.

To the east of the pass, one of Europe's great bouldering areas is found and climbers come from afar just for that. When it snows what better thing to do than make the most of good friction at this 'cool' location!

FROM TOP

▷ Michi Tresch and his dog Mara.
   Michi Tresch, unnamed arête (6b).
   Jvan Tresch, *Madrugada* (8a+).

THAILAND
PHI PHI ISLAND

Phi Phi Island, or Koh Phi Phi, was one of Thailand's first major climbing destinations. Over the years it also became an exceedingly popular tourist destination known for exceptional snorkelling and diving. As tourism boomed here in the late 90's climbers increasingly turned their attention to other areas such as Railay and Ton Sai, just two and a half hours ferry ride away.

These images were created prior to the devastating December 2004 tsunami which killed hundreds here and destroyed many buildings. Yet, incredibly, after little more than six months so much rebuilding work had been done that the island was reopened and tourists encouraged once again.

Prior to the tsunami, Phi Phi was seeing a resurgence of climbing after many of the mid-grade single and multi-pitch limestone routes had been re-equipped with new stainless steel bolts. Perhaps climbing can play a significant role in the island's future.

FROM TOP
◩ Patrick Turner, pitch three
   Happy Banana (6c), Hin Taak Wall.
   Heading back from Hin Taak Wall.
   Phi Phi sunrise.

➡ Rachel Carr,
Travels With My Aunt (6a),
Hin Taak Wall.

THAILAND

PHRA-NANG

When climbers start dreaming of warm weather holidays it is little wonder the Phra Nang Peninsular so often ends up top of the list. The hundreds of single and multi-pitch sport-climbs and the beaches (to help rest aching muscles and frayed nerves) are obvious attractions. Numerous restaurants and bars, and one's own private bungalow (as luxurious or as cheap as you like), have helped complete the package and make this a fun place to hang out. It's a friendly and vibrant scene. Some climbers return year after year.

The area's geology has given climbers much to be thankful for — aside from just the creation of steep tufa-dripped limestone of course. The main beaches of Railay and Ton Sai on the peninsular are reached by boat, not road, which adds a little to the remoteness but greatly to the place's appeal.

➔ Monique Forestier,
Burnt Offerings (7a+), Melting Wall.

↑ Grant Rowbottom, *Tantrum* (8a+), Ton Sai.

↗ Grant Rowbottom, *No Name* (8a), Ton Sai.

→ Rachel Carr, pitch four *Humanality* (6a+, 6b, 6b+, 6b, 6a), Ton Sai.

Chris Savage, *Jai Dum* (8b), Ton Sai.
Approaching Rai Lay West.

UNITED KINGDOM
DORSET

The Dorset coast is blessed with a relatively mild climate for England. This has done more than just enhance the popularity of the sea-cliff climbing here; most notably at Swanage (for trad and sport) and Portland (for sport). The warm weather and summer ocean currents have also enabled the overhanging sea cliffs to become something of a global spring-board for the refinement of the Deep-Water Soloing style. The style has obvious attractions and has long been a fun pastime for many.

Here, in the late 1990's, a few bold locals started by soloing some of the bolted limestone sport-routes that were wildly overhanging above water. They were soon pushing the limits and began scouring the coastline for steep, previously unclimbed rock.

Pushing it, DWS style, is not as simple as it might seem. It is more than just the fact that as falls get bigger, water becomes a hard and unforgiving medium. And it is more than just the need for warm water, the right tides and swells, rescue swimmers and other measures, and learning how to fall safely. Those involved with the development of this style have learned the hard way. They have worked out how to manage many of the identified safety issues. But this style can still remain serious stuff.

→ Dave Pickford soloing *Davy Jones's Locker* (E4 6a), Conner Cove.

UNITED KINGDOM

LLANBERIS

The town of Llanberis in North Wales is a major centre for climbing with a wide assortment of climbing areas nearby. A truly unique climbing experience can be found in the abandoned quarries that are cut into the hillsides above the town. The quarries exist thanks to the thousands of hardworking Welshmen who, over many decades, toiled in harsh and often dangerous conditions extracting the slate. Over seventeen thousand workers were employed at the peak of the industry in the 1890's. The last large quarry closed in 1969 and climbing took off in the 1980's. They are interesting sociologically to explore.

The local climbing ethics are also interesting. Traditionally protected climbs are most common though bolting exists. Some of the slabs are real mind trips with bolting so spaced that a falling climber might be lucky not to 'hit the deck'. When it comes to safety most climbers don't seem to mind a few bolts here and there — but local ethics have helped ensure that any further modification of the rock has been minimal. Simply, climbers have largely resisted the temptation to 'chip' additional holds in the rock. Which is significant when you consider that these cliffs are the direct result of heavy industry and modification by man; it would be all too easy to say 'it is man-made anyway'. This is indeed a unique and challenging playground; the ethics help keep it that way — and the climbers have earned much respect.

→ Ben Heason, *Slipstream* (E6 6b), Rainbow Slab.

⬆ Steve McClure examining the old slate cutting room.

⬈ Steve McClure, *The Very Big and the Very Small* (8c), Rainbow Slab.

➡ Steve McClure, *The Very Big and the Very Small*.

◄ Ben Heason, ***Comes
The Dervish*** (E3 5c),
Vivian Quarry.

➡ Ben Heason soloing
Seams The Same
(E1 5b), Seamstress Slab.

UNITED KINGDOM
PEAK DISTRICT

There are often more factors than just climbing which lure climbers to live in a particular area. But if the size of a local scene is any indication of a climbing area's allure, judging by the masses of climbers living in the city of Sheffield, the Peak District has an irresistible charm.

The gritstone and limestone crags scattered around this region have differing characteristics — and associated ethics — which have made for an enormous diversity of climbing. The gritstone crags (or "Edges" as they are called here) remain great for trad climbing due to the staunch ethic of keeping them bolt-free. The gritstone can pack a punch; and what the Edges lack in stature has been more than compensated for by being the scene of some of the most exceptionally bold climbing around. Meanwhile, on the limestone crags sport-climbing has been embraced, enabling technical climbing to help push world standards along. Bouldering is big around here too.

The diversity of climbing has done more than just require climbers to understand several grading systems. It has meant there are new playthings for climbers as their abilities and interests change over time. It is a potent mix which has influenced the lives and lifestyles of many.

⬆ Stanage Edge.
↗ Steve McClure, *Mutation* (9a), Raven Tor.

Steve McClure,
Mecca (8b+),
Raven Tor.

◧ Lucy Creamer, *Tales of Yankee Power* (E5 6a), High Tor.
◩ Mike Weeks, *Chequers Buttress* (HVS 5b), Froggatt Edge.
⬆ Lucy Creamer, *Flying Buttress Direct* (HVS 5b), Stanage Edge.

UNITED KINGDOM

PEMBROKE

Perhaps climbing on sea-cliffs has a special appeal because they make us feel as far away from it all as can be. Possibly it's the attraction of the ocean and beaches nearby and the notion that we might get a chance to enjoy them. Or it could just be for good climbing on one of a thousand plus routes. Whatever the reasons, Pembroke (in southwest Wales) has a real appeal — as the crowds on 'bank holiday' suggest.

The rock here is ultra strong and featured in a way limestone rarely is. The plentiful small cracks accept perfect placements of natural protection making this one of the best trad crags around. Though it nearly didn't work out that way.

Years ago a few climbers started placing bolts on some routes for increased convenience and safety. Others disagreed with that approach, arguing bolts were not necessary given that good natural protection could often be found. They said that if it couldn't be climbed without bolts then it was better left for the future — or just left unclimbed. So they removed the bolts. After some debate it was eventually widely agreed that this cliff would remain bolt free. The agreement reached here has had significant implications, becoming in some ways a benchmark for the way crags are now officially designated either 'sport' or 'trad' country-wide. Ultimately resulting in far fewer arguments!

⊿ A view towards St Govan's Head.

➡ Mike Weeks, **Herod** (E1 5b),
Mother Carey's Kitchen.

➜ Simon Tappin,
Fitz-In (E5 6a),
Huntsman's Leap.

↑ Tim Emmett soloing *The Gateaux Thief*, (E6 6b), Stennis Ford.

↗ Mikey Robertson, *Living On Air* (E8 6c), Stennis Ford.

→ Adrian Baxter, *San Simeon* (E8 6c), Hollow Caves Bay.

⬆ Trevor Massiah, **The Hypocrite** (E3 6a), Pembroke North.
➡ Trevor Massiah, **Kitten Claws** (E3 5c), Pembroke North.

⬆ Charlie Woodburn, *Brazen Buttress* (E2 5b), Mother Carey's Kitchen.

⬈ Mike Weeks, *Sunlover Direct* (E3 5c), Trevallen.

UNITED STATES OF AMERICA
BISHOP

Sitting in a rain shadow east of California's Sierra Nevada, the town of Bishop often enjoys conditions conducive to great bouldering even while it snows on the range. Snow then, is a signal for climbers to head out and explore the seemingly endless hillsides of beautifully sculptured quartz monzonite blocks of the Buttermilk region. This includes the Giant Peabody Boulders and countless outlying areas, such as the Pollen Grains and Sherman Acres. Whereas the volcanic tuff at the Happy and Sad boulders has also weathered into interesting shapes, providing hours of entertainment on its many sinker pockets.

Bishop is also a good launching pad for the stunning array of alpine climbing in the Sierras above, while Owens River Gorge offers good sport climbing nearby. And adding to the outdoor delights the Mammoth Lakes region, a forty minute drive to the north, has several natural spas to soothe sore tips and toes.

Hidetaka Suzuki, *Secret of Beehive* (V5), Buttermilk Boulders.

Lisa Rands, Sherman Acres.

↑ Henrik Janson,
The Iron Man Traverse
(V4), Buttermilk Boulders.

➜ Hidetaka Suzuki,
Hand to Hand Combat
(V7), Happy Boulders.

UNITED STATES OF AMERICA
INDIAN CREEK

From Moab, an hour's drive south through Utah's expansive cowboy country will get you to the North and South Six Shooter Peaks and the wide open valleys of Indian Creek. Here sandstone escarpments are split by the most parallel-sided cracks imaginable. Some so parallel that a climber may need to place ten pieces of protection, all the same size, all in the one pitch.

The rock is friendly and smooth, but as there are few face holds it is the width of the crack that determines which body parts can best be jammed into them to gain a hold. Some cracks come in 'handy' widths — which best fit fingers, hands, or fists. On the wider 'off-width' cracks some extraordinary techniques are employed: hands or fists are stacked against each other — and the rock — and squeezed to prevent sliding out. Even jamming a foot overhead might be the key to allow a stacked hand-and-fist jamb to be reset a few inches higher. These steep wide off-widths demand a committed fight. They are relished by only a devoted few.

There are a thousand routes here, though few at easy grades. With many of the cracks long and sustained, they are unforgiving to imperfect technique but that also makes them perfect for refining skills. The climbing has a real purity which attracts enthusiasts from all over, for Indian Creek is crack-climbing paradise.

↗ Desert flowers.
➡ The rack for **Belly Full of Bad Berries**.

→ John Varco, *Johnny Cat*
(5.11d), Cat Wall.

UNITED STATES OF AMERICA
LAS VEGAS

The Nevada desert seems an unlikely place to find one of the world's biggest cities for gambling and live entertainment, but there you have it: Las Vegas, in all its neon glory and its notorious casino strip, where punters come from all over to toss their money away. The odds might also seem against it, but not much more than a coin's throw from downtown Vegas, climbers can find a jackpot of their own on the desert sandstone of Red Rocks.

There are thousands of routes here. One could climb high quality sport-routes for weeks without ever realising the area's full extent. But the mountain and canyon walls nearby are also major destinations in their own right. They have multi-pitch consumer-friendly outings and committing adventures up to fifteen pitches long. And if all the sandstone at Red Rocks isn't enough, there are also hundreds of sport-climbs on the steep limestone at Mount Charleston — some of which are among the hardest in the country. It all adds up to make Vegas, for rock climbers, pretty much a sure bet.

↗ Bill McLemore,
The Sissy Traverse (5.13b),
The Gallery, Red Rocks.

nd endless
around Moab,
uld be the
ten it is.
e hundreds of
Fisher Towers,
t some of the
estination.
many others
es from
ut the same
mmon and

pe you would
bing around
n particular
ch quality
House is
oulder"
g twenty
high cave.

⬆ Greg Child, pitch one **Excommunication** (12b, 12a, 13a, 11b, 10d), The Priest, Castle Valley.

➡ Greg Child, pitch two **Excommunication** with Renee Globis belaying.

⬆ Monique Forestier atop the Corkscrew Summit, **Stolen Chimney** (5 pitches, 5.11a) on Ancient Art, Fisher Towers.
⬆ Lisa Hathaway, **Fine Mexican Boyfriend** (5.11d), Mill Creek.

FROM LEFT
⬆ Annie Overling, **The Birth Canal**, The Crack House.
John Varco, project, near The Crack House.
Jonathan Thesenga, **Full Crack House**.

→ Tate Rees, *Full Crack House* (V9 or 5.13a/b), The Crack House.

UNITED STATES OF AMERICA
YOSEMITE

Regardless of expectations, it would still be hard for Valley first-timers not to be awed on first sighting these big-walls. For here we have — El Capitan with its thousand vertical metres perfectly placed centre-stage in the Valley; the proudly positioned Half Dome with its enormous walls; and many other massive expanses of clean granite scattered around this dazzling glacier-cleaved valley. Also close by is Tuolumne Meadows with its numerous glorious golden domes giving far more than a simple summertime escape from the Valley.

Yosemite's oft proclaimed status as one of the world's best and most significant climbing areas is not without justification. Stories of epic early ascents which took many weeks are part of the area's intriguing history. Several items of equipment widely considered essential by climbers today were originally developed to specifically tackle these big walls. The American grading system was devised here but at the time, with 5.9 as the top grade, it was unforeseen how climbing would change and standards would rise!

Climbing standards still regularly get pushed here: in aid, free and speed big-wall styles. It's all grand testimony to the great skill, boldness and dedication of the climbers and to the inspiration and exceptional climbing that these routes provide. Valley climbing is far more than just big walls and hard routes though, moderate ultra-classics abound too. Climbers come from all over and when they arrive have to stand in line to take a ticket for the privilege of pitching their tents amongst the bear-proof food-boxes of the zero-star "Camp 4". But that's okay... this is climbing's Mecca.

← Half Dome.

↖ El Capitan.

→ David Bloom, third
last pitch (5.11b)
Golden Gate (41 pitches,
5.13b), El Capitan.

Following page: Cedar
Wright, **Notes From
The Underground** (5.12d),
Taft Point, with El Capitan
in the background.

This and following pages:
Photos from record
speed ascent (two hours,
31 minutes, 20 seconds)
of *Zodiac* (VI, 5.11 A3),
El Capitan.

← Alex Huber leading pitch 13.

Zodiac speed ascent photos continued: As Thomas Huber 'jumars' pitch 14 (left) with his rope attached to one bolt, there is slack in the system (centre) before it connects to Alex leading pitch 15 (right).

→ Hans Florine,
Fun Terminal (5.12a),
Killer Pillar.

◄ Heidi Wirtz, pitch two
Shipoopi! (5.11d),
Medlicott Dome,
Tuolumne Meadows.

→ Stefan Schiller,
pitch two **Bachar-Yerian**
(5.11c), Medlicott Dome,
Tuolumne Meadows.

Following page:
David Bloom, pitch one
Shipoopi! (5.11aR),
Medlicott Dome,
Tuolumne Meadows.

PHOTOGRAPHIC NOTES

Photography and climbing are two different skills which don't necessarily combine. I'm often asked questions by photographers or climbers wanting to know more about one or the other. It might seem obvious, but in the same way climbing is dangerous, photographing it also has hazards. The warning on page 192 applies to photographers too.

In climbing photography, your climbing skills keep you alive. There are enough hazards already so it is important to be competent in a cliff environment before adding the distraction of a camera into the equation. To be unprepared or incompetent is to invite the consequences of Darwinism! Scrambling around near cliffs unroped is dangerous. Loose rocks can be dislodged. There are unknowns.

Abseiling or jumaring, or just swinging around, can cause a rope to cut where it rubs against sharp rock. Manufacturers make static ropes for good reason and I have a strong preference for using one when photographing from abseil. I like to use rope protectors a lot.

I use a tripod when I can, but most of the photos here were taken from abseil. I use a chest harness to help reduce camera shake which occurs in awkward positions. Sometimes I'll abseil down in different places and see how it looks through a lens to decide the best angles. It's frustrating to abseil down and find you are metres from the best angle and running out of time.

Preparation puts you in the right position so when the climber is going for it you can just blast away with your finger on the motor drive. It's an action sport, things happen quickly. I had about an hour on the abseil rope before the Hubers came into view during a speed ascent of Zodiac. In this time I worked out where I was going to be, which lenses I was going to use, when I was

going to change them, and when I was going to jumar between angles.

The majority of photos in this book were taken during serious attempts or successful ascents. A climber may attempt a climb several times giving opportunities to shoot from another angle. I do not ask climbers to get on routes that are unreasonable for them to attempt or to adopt a particular pose. However it is worth considering how a route will look at different times of day and in different light.

35mm SLR's give the best balance of speed, size, strength, and clarity. I've used Nikon for decades and the F100 model these last few years. I used to use a 20-35 zoom but now favour fixed focal length prime lenses throughout the range as they are brighter and sharper. My favourites are the 16, 20, 35, 85, 135, and 180mm. In the last few years I've replaced the 180mm with a 1.4x tele-converter used with the 135mm, giving a 189mm manual focus lens. This is a good option when weight is an issue so I go that way a lot.

With the exception of the rare use of a slight warming filter when shooting in deep shade, I do not use filters and they were not used for any images in this book. Modern cameras are very good at automatically determining exposure but I mostly use spot metering in manual mode as this is very precise and gives complete control.

My favourite film is Fuji Velvia (50 ASA), which I rate at 40 ASA. I like its fine grain and vibrant colours. Generally when I need a bit of extra speed I use the 100 ASA version. Also Fuji Provia can help reduce over-saturation in orangey light before sunset. I am not sponsored by any camera or film company.

Digital photography has come a long way but it's not there for me yet. I also like the physical aspect of film.

Digital manipulation of images is another matter altogether. A manipulated image is not an image of a real moment. While it is normal to use a computer program to crop, clean off dust and other imperfections, and to optimise (or even enhance) the reproduction of tones and colours, it is another thing altogether to add or create wholesale sections of images, and present them without declaring it.

Manipulation degrades photography: it undermines confidence in the image. You don't have to capture the moment. Knowing an image is manipulated changes the way I feel about it. None of the images in this book are digitally manipulated.

I've enjoyed photographing the diversity of modern climbing. There are images of cutting-edge achievements and new standards being set, but often it has been the classic of the crag, or a route tackling a beautiful or unusual formation, that has caught my eye.

My favourite images are those which capture the visual elements of both action and setting without compromising either. As a photographer this is a challenge. Blending both into one composition results in a satisfying and more meaningful image. It's no coincidence that those images are the ones which best reflect my philosophy of climbing — and why I love it so much.

→ Chris Sharma, **No Future** (8c+), Ceuse, France.

GLOSSARY

CLIMBING STYLES

AID CLIMBING Mechanically assisted climbing. Body weight is supported by protection, or other equipment, and used to directly 'aid' upwards progress.

ALPINE CLIMBING Climbing higher altitude peaks or mountains, commonly involving climbing snow and ice.

BOULDERING Unroped climbing, close to the ground.

DEEP WATER SOLOING (DWS) Climbing without a rope or protection above deep water, usually the ocean.

FLASH To lead climb a route on the very first attempt but where the climber has some prior knowledge of the difficulties or sequence of moves.

FREE CLIMBING Using hands and feet (and any other body part) to climb the rock's natural features. The rope and protection are there but not weighted or used to directly 'aid' the ascent.

LEAD The first person of a party climbing a route. The 'leader' clips the rope into protection points along the way whilst belayed from below.

MIXED CLIMBING Climbing on rock and ice on the same pitch.

ONSIGHT To lead climb a route making a successful ascent on the first attempt. The climber has no prior knowledge of the specific difficulties of the route. This is widely considered the best lead climbing style.

PINKPOINT A redpoint ascent but with protection pre-placed. This term is considered redundant in many parts of the world particularly in sport climbing.

REDPOINT A style of climbing, widely regarded as the minimum standard for claiming a 'free' ascent. The route must be led without a fall or any assistance from the rope or protection.

SECOND The climber who ascends a route or pitch after the lead climber. They are belayed from above.

SOLO To climb alone. In free climbing this means without a rope (free solo). In aid climbing a rope is used (aid solo).

SPORT CLIMBING Where permanent fixed protection (commonly bolts) is utilised thereby allowing for an emphasis on gymnastic movement.

TOP-ROPE To climb with the rope belayed or anchored from above.

TRADITIONAL CLIMBING aka **TRAD** Climbing characterised by the placing of removable protection (slings, nuts, camming devices).

CLIMBING TERMS

ABSEIL aka **RAPPEL** Method for descending a rope.

BELAY The system using a rope to arrest a climber's fall. Includes the anchors and stance that the belayer uses, and involves using a friction (belay) device to lock-off the rope.

BELAYER The person using the rope to provide safety to someone who is climbing.

BIG WALL A big cliff face offering particularly long routes, possibly requiring numerous days to climb.

BOLT A construction bolt fixed into a pre-drilled hole, used as a permanent anchor or protection point.

BOMBER A particularly dependable gear placement.

CHICKENHEAD A protruding knob of rock.

CHIPPING The deliberate action of modifying the rock to create holds where they do not naturally exist. This is considered completely unethical in most areas of the world.

CRACK A fracture or split in the rock.

CRAG A smaller cliff or set of cliffs.

CRAMPON Metal spikes which attach to boots for gaining a grip on ice.

CRANK To pull hard on a hand hold.

CRUX The most difficult section of the climb.

DRYTOOLING To climb on rock using ice climbing tools (crampons and ice axes).

EDGES Small handholds. In England it is also the name given to some small outcrops of rock (e.g. Stanage Edge).

ETHICS Widely accepted standards of conduct at an area, particularly relating to actions which may damage the rock.

EXPOSED, EXPOSURE In mountaineering: being susceptible to the elements (heat, cold, wind or rain). In climbing: being a long way above the ground, often resulting in an enhanced feeling of nervousness.

FACE A steep open section of cliff.

GEAR See protection

GRADE A subjective rating of the difficulty of a climb. There are different grading systems for aid climbs, free climbs and boulder problems.

GROUND-UP To climb from ground level without previous inspection or preparation from above (such as from abseil). As opposed to top-down.

JAM, JAMMING OR JAMBING A climbing technique where a hand, foot or other body part is squeezed inside a crack to provide a hold.

JUG A very large hold.

JUMAR A brand of a rope-ascending device. **Jumaring** is a generic term for the technique of ascending fixed ropes using ascenders.

MULTI-PITCH A longer route which has more than a single pitch of climbing.

OFFWIDTH A wide crack, awkward to climb.

OVERHANG An extra steep (overhanging) section of rock.

PITCH The section of climbing between two belays, not longer than the length of the rope.

PROJECT A climb which has been attempted but not yet properly free-climbed.

PROTECTION, PRO Various types of equipment placed in rock features to stop a falling climber. **Natural** or **traditional** protection is removable (non-permanent). **Fixed** protection is anchor points permanently fixed in the rock (includes bolts or pitons).

POCKET Holes in the rock face, used for hand or foot holds.

PUMPY Strenuous climbing.

RACK A selection of traditional protection carried on a climb.

ROOF A horizontal, or near horizontal, overhanging section of rock.

RUN-OUT The distance the lead climber is above their last piece of protection. A run-out climb has big fall potential.

SLAB A large off-vertical span of rock: seemingly featureless, it is often climbed with balance and friction techniques.

TOP-DOWN Using abseil or a top-rope to access, inspect, practice or prepare the route before attempting to climb.

TRAVERSE To climb sideways, horizontally.

TUFA A fin-like rock formation found in limestone.

TYROLEAN TRAVERSE To slide along a rope fixed between two formations which are elevated and separated by a void.